DaMarcus Beasley

Soccer Star Sensation

Carol Parenzan Smalley

Mitchell Lane
PUBLISHERS

P.O. Box 196
Hockessin, Delaware 19707
Visit us on the web: www.mitchelllane.com
Comments? email us: mitchelllane@mitchelllane.com

Printing   1   2   3   4   5   6   7   8

A Robbie Reader
No Hands Allowed

Brandi Chastain   Brian McBride   **DaMarcus Beasley**
David Beckham   Freddy Adu   Josh Wolff
Landon Donovan

Library of Congress Cataloging-in-Publication Data
Smalley, Carol Parenzan, 1960–
    DaMarcus Beasley / by Carol Parenzan Smalley.
        p. cm. – (A Robbie reader. No hands allowed)
    Includes bibliographical references and index.
    ISBN 1-58415-387-3 (library bound)
    1. Beasley, DaMarcus, 1982–Juvenile literature. 2. Soccer players–United States–Biography–Juvenile literature. I. Title. II. Series.
GV942.7.B395S62 2006
796.334'092–dc22
                                                                                                    2005014904

ABOUT THE AUTHOR: Carol Parenzan Smalley is a writer and an educator. She has authored numerous books for the educational market, including a five-book series on government for Perfection Learning, a book on the food pyramid for Scholastic Library, and several other titles for Mitchell Lane, including a Robbie Reader biography about Henry Hudson and a four-book extreme sports adventure series. She created an American Sign Language guide and flashcard set for Barnes and Noble. She is the former managing editor of several business Web sites and publications. She is an instructor of an online course called Writing for Children, which she teaches through more than 1,000 colleges and universities around the world. She is also an instructor in small business in the classroom and online. With an engineering degree from The Pennsylvania State University, she is currently studying the art of paper engineering and 3-D pop-up design. And her competitive spirit has surfaced once more, as she has returned to the pool as a master's level swimmer. Her favorite stroke is butterfly. She and her family live in a log cabin in the Adirondack Mountains of upstate New York.

PHOTO CREDITS: Cover–Peter Aiken/WireImage; pp. 1, 3–Kim Jae-Hwan/AFP/Getty Images; pp. 4, 8, 10–courtesy of Diane Small/Bradenton Academy; p. 13–Michael Stahlschmidt/MLS/Allsport/Getty Images; p. 14–Stephen Dunn/Getty Images; p. 17–Alice Leafblad/SSP/Time Life Pictures/Getty Images; p. 18–Gary M. Prior/Getty Images; p. 21 (top)–Roberto Schmidt/AFP/Getty Images; p. 21 (bottom)–Ben Radford/Getty Images; p. 22–Jamie McDonald/Getty Images; p. 24–Sharon Beck; p. 26 (top)–Jonathan Ferrey/Getty Images; p. 26 (bottom)–Jim McIsaac/Getty Images.

ACKNOWLEDGMENTS: The following story has been thoroughly researched, and to the best of our knowledge, represents a true story. While every possible effort has been made to ensure accuracy, the publisher will not assume liability for damages caused by inaccuracies in the data, and makes no warranty on the accuracy of the information contained herein. This story has not been authorized nor endorsed by DaMarcus Beasley nor anyone associated with DaMarcus Beasley.

APR   2008

CONELY BRANCH

TABLE OF CONTENTS

Chapter One
A Childhood Dream 5

Chapter Two
An Athlete and a Student 9

Chapter Three
A Pro at Age 16 15

Chapter Four
The World Cup 19

Chapter Five
Exported to Europe 23

Chronology 27–28
Glossary 28–29
Find Out More 30–31
Index 32

When DaMarcus was a little boy, his father bought him a soccer ball. Since that time, he has wanted to become a famous soccer player.

A Childhood Dream

DaMarcus Lamont Beasley was a skinny five-year-old kid. He liked playing sports with his friends. They played basketball, baseball, and football. DaMarcus may have been thin, but he was fast. He was a natural athlete.

One day his father, Henry, gave DaMarcus and his older brother, Jamar, a soccer ball. They had never played soccer before. Their friends told them that soccer was for girls. They did not care.

DaMarcus and Jamar practiced together. They learned how to handle the ball. They passed it back and forth using their feet. DaMarcus used his left foot to kick the ball far. They bounced the ball off their heads. Soccer became very important to the brothers. They played on soccer teams with other kids.

5

DaMarcus's parents, Henry and Joetta Beasley (shown here), have always encouraged and supported DaMarcus's soccer playing.

At the time, soccer was not popular in the United States. Many soccer stars lived in Europe. DaMarcus dreamed that one day he would play soccer in Europe.

His mother, Joetta, bought videotapes of **international** (in-ter-NAH-shuh-nul) soccer matches. DaMarcus and Jamar watched them. DaMarcus liked to watch Michel Platini. Platini played for the French national soccer team. He was white. DaMarcus was African-American. People told DaMarcus that soccer was not a sport for African-Americans. But he did not believe them.

Some people thought that DaMarcus was too small to be a **professional** (pruh-FEH-shuh-nul) athlete. He did not care. He thought that size did not matter. He thought it was more important to play the game well. He practiced hard to be the best.

DaMarcus's dream to play soccer in Europe came true. By 2004, he was a professional soccer star for a winning team. DaMarcus and his sport had grown. The skinny boy born on May 24, 1982, in Fort Wayne, Indiana, had become a European soccer star.

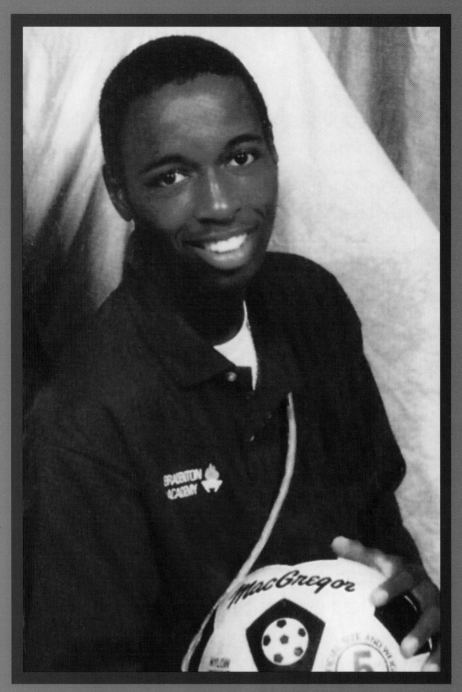

In his senior year of high school, DaMarcus received several soccer awards. He was named the Parade All-American High School Co-Player of the Year.

An Athlete and a Student

Soccer was important for DaMarcus. School was important, too. DaMarcus was both a star athlete and a good student.

DaMarcus played soccer and basketball at South Side High School in Fort Wayne. He and Jamar played together on the high school soccer team for two years.

DaMarcus played in his first international competition when he was only 14 years old. He was a member of the U.S. **Under-16** National Team. They played against France on May 20, 1997. DaMarcus celebrated his fifteenth birthday four days later.

Later that year, DaMarcus moved away from his family to live in Florida. He trained

DaMarcus excelled in the classroom and on the soccer field. His school, Bradenton Academy, named an award in his honor.

there with the U.S. Under-17 National Team. The team practiced in the afternoons at the IMG (International Management Group) Academy. In the mornings, DaMarcus went to school at Bradenton Preparatory Academy. He studied hard and got good grades.

DaMarcus wanted to be a normal student. He had fun with his friends. He played on the school's soccer team. He was the team's captain. He thought that everyone on the school soccer team should play. Every team member was important.

In 1999, DaMarcus and his under-17 teammates stood out at the **FIFA** (Fédération Internationale de Football Association) World Championships. The team finished fourth. DaMarcus was named Man of the Match two times. He was awarded the Silver Ball as the second most valuable player. The most valuable player award went to his teammate, Landon Donovan.

DaMarcus scored one of the most spectacular goals of the **tournament**. He used his quick speed and fast moves. He **volleyed** the ball up the field for 30 yards. The crowd went wild.

DaMarcus had the chance to leave school and play professional soccer. He decided to stay in school. He graduated with his class of 47 students. Nickelodeon came to take pictures of him on graduation day. DaMarcus

was embarrassed. He felt that the day should be about his entire class. He did not want to be different.

The school made an award in his honor. It is called the DaMarcus Beasley Leadership Award. It is given to a Bradenton Academy senior who works hard in the classroom and on the sports field.

DaMarcus received many awards as a student athlete. He was chosen for the 1998 NSCAA High School All-America Team. (NSCAA is the National Soccer Coaches Association of America.) He was named the Parade All-American High School Co-Player of the Year in 1999. And he was named the Florida Soccer Player of the Year.

But something even bigger happened to him his senior year. DaMarcus signed a contract to play professional soccer. He was one step closer to his dream.

DaMarcus was selected to play professional soccer with the Chicago (Illinois) Fire team. He was one step closer to his dream.

DaMarcus was the youngest MLS player to be voted one of the Best XI. Here he holds a trophy during the MLS Gala Awards Ceremony.

A Pro at Age 16

DaMarcus made history in 1999 when he was 16 years and 10 months old. He signed a **Major League Soccer** (MLS) contract. He became the youngest MLS player. Since then, other players have broken that record.

At first, DaMarcus was signed to the Los Angeles, California, Galaxy team. Before he had a chance to lace up his shoes, he moved to the Chicago Fire in Illinois.

In his first year, DaMarcus started in eleven games. He scored six goals.

DaMarcus made a lot of money for his age. He earned $150,000 a year to play soccer. He drove a fancy car. He ate at the best restaurants. He had his own apartment in Chicago. He was happy to play professional soccer in the United States. But he never forgot about the European soccer players. They made much more money than players in the United States. In Europe, soccer players were heroes.

DaMarcus was a midfielder for the Chicago Fire for five seasons. In 2000, *World Soccer* magazine named him one of the Top 100 Rising Stars. He was one of the ten youngest players on the list.

In 2001, both he and Jamar were on the same team. His parents traveled to Chicago to watch the brothers play.

DaMarcus was named to the MLS All-Star teams for three straight years (2001, 2002, and 2003). In 2001, he was named the U.S. Soccer Young Male Athlete of the Year. In 2003, at the age of 21, he was the youngest player ever voted to the MLS Best XI. (There are eleven players on a soccer team. The Best XI are the top eleven players in the country.) He scored 14 goals and had 17 assists during 83 MLS games while he played for Chicago.

DaMarcus liked to mix up his game. Sometimes he made simple moves. Sometimes

Jamar Beasley (shown here) played for the Chicago Fire just like his brother, DaMarcus.

he did fancy footwork. He liked to take chances. His coaches saw him as a two-way player. He played both offense and defense.

DaMarcus weighed only 137 pounds. He was 5 feet 8 inches tall. He was still skinny, but he was still fast.

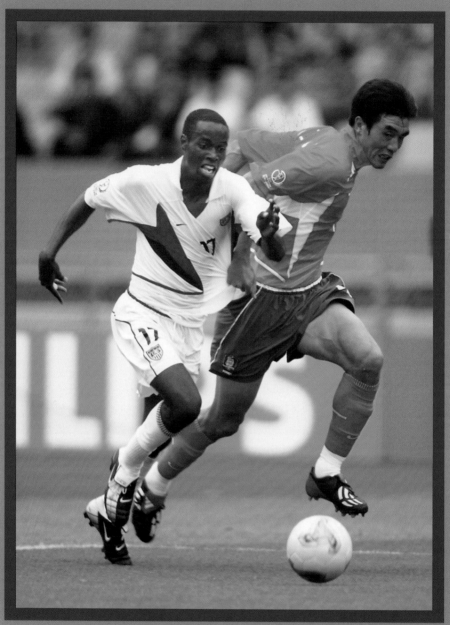

DaMarcus uses his speed to run past South Korean player, Jin Cheul Choi, during an FIFA World Cup Finals match.

CHAPTER FOUR

The World Cup

DaMarcus was not just a professional soccer player. He was an American who could play on national soccer teams. The national teams played against the European teams DaMarcus dreamed about.

The U.S. Under-20 National Team played in the 2001 **CONCACAF qualifying** (see glossary) tournament. In this tournament, the best soccer teams from North America, South America, and the Caribbean islands play against one another. The winning teams go on to play in the **World Cup**. DaMarcus was named the most valuable player on the U.S. team for the qualifying tournament.

DaMarcus was the youngest player on the 2002 World Cup Team. He played with African-

American teammates Eddie Pope, Tony Sanneh, and Cobi Jones. This was the most African-Americans ever to play on the U.S. team.

DaMarcus was a starting player in the World Cup competitions against Portugal and South Korea. He was a substitute player against Poland.

The U.S. played well but did not win the World Cup that year. They lost to Germany in the **quarterfinals**.

DaMarcus remembered his childhood dream when he played against these other countries. He still dreamed of playing in Europe.

The U.S. 2002 World Cup Team: top row left to right—Brad Friedel, Eddie Pope, Jeff Agoos, Brian McBride, Tony Sanneh, and David Regis; bottom row left to right—Clint Mathis, Earnie Stewart, DaMarcus Beasley, Chris Armas, and Cobi Jones.

DaMarcus tries to shield the ball from Maciej Murawski of Poland during the 2002 FIFA World Cup match held in South Korea.

DaMarcus's dream was to play soccer (called football) in Europe. In 2004, he started playing with PSV Eindhoven, one of the best teams in the Netherlands. As an American, DaMarcus still represents the United States in international competitions.

Exported to Europe

DaMarcus's dream finally came true in 2004. In Europe and other countries, soccer is called **football**. (The word *soccer* comes from the letters *s-o-c* in the name *association football*.) DaMarcus went to Europe to play "football." He began playing for a Dutch team called PSV Eindhoven. It is one of the best teams in the Netherlands' professional soccer league.

Soccer is different in Europe. The game is faster. Many fans come to the matches. DaMarcus played his first match for Eindhoven in front of 65,000 people.

Many in the crowd whistled or booed at him. Some made other rude noises. There were not many African-American soccer players in Europe. DaMarcus was not used to this **racism**.

This is a map of the Netherlands. DaMarcus lives in Eindhoven (shown in red) and plays for its soccer team.

He thought that fans should judge him on how well he played, and not on the color of his skin.

Over time, the fans grew to love him. So did his teammates.

In 2005, he was settling down in Eindhoven. He misses his family and friends in the United States. He calls his parents each week. Sometimes they fly to Europe to watch him play. Sometimes they watch his matches over the Internet. He e-mails his friends. He watches American DVDs and listens to hip-hop, rap, and reggae music.

Some of his teammates call him "McDonald" for one of the fast-food restaurants that America is known for. Others call him "Jitterbug" for his quick moves on the soccer field. And the fans now call him "Kampioen" (champion).

DaMarcus has helped his team win many games. In his first season, he scored 12 goals in 42 games. In 2005, the Eindhoven team won the Dutch league championship. They beat Vitesse Arnhem 3-0.

DaMarcus's dream to play soccer in Europe came true. He wants to help other young American soccer players realize their dreams too. Most importantly, DaMarcus believes in healthy living. He visits schools to talk about the hazards that come from smoking tobacco.

Someday he wants to open a soccer stadium and children's training camp in his hometown of Fort Wayne. But for now, he just wants to play soccer.

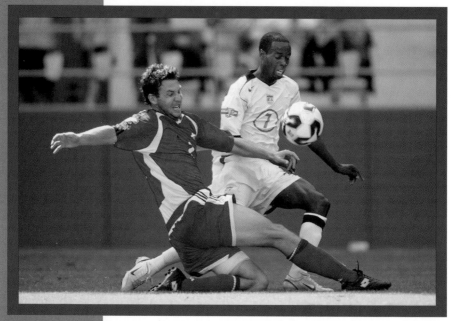

CHAPTER FIVE

DaMarcus crosses the ball for an assist past Adam Braz of Canada in the preliminary rounds of the CONCACAF Gold Cup on July 9, 2005.

DaMarcus and Jermaine Taylor of Jamaica collide during the CONCACAF quarterfinal match on July 16, 2005.

1982 DaMarcus Lamont Beasley is born on May 24 in Fort Wayne, Indiana.

1987 He receives his first soccer ball from his father, Henry Beasley.

1997 DaMarcus plays his first international soccer match against France; he moves to Florida to train with the Under-17 National Team and attends Bradenton Preparatory Academy.

1998 He is named to the NSCAA High School All-America Team.

1999 He is named Parade All-American High School Co-Player of the Year and Florida Soccer Player of the Year. He graduates from Bradenton Preparatory Academy. He wins the Silver Ball in the FIFA Under-17 World Championships and signs a professional soccer contract with Major League Soccer.

2000 His rookie year, he plays with the Chicago Fire. *World Soccer* magazine names him one of the Top 100 Rising Stars.

2001 He plays with brother Jamar on the Chicago Fire. DaMarcus is named the

U.S. Soccer Young Male Athlete of the Year.

2002 DaMarcus plays on the U.S. World Cup Team.

2003 He is voted to the MLS Best XI.

2004 He signs a contract with PSV Eindhoven to play "football" and moves to Europe.

2005 He is part of the PSV Eindhoven team that wins the Dutch league championship.

GLOSSARY

CONCACAF—the Confederation of North, Central American and Caribbean Association Football. This group is in charge of soccer for countries in these regions. The United States is a member of CONCACAF.

FIFA—the Fédération Internationale de Football Association. This group is in charge of world football (soccer) and is headquartered in Lucerne, Switzerland.

football—the international term for soccer.

international (in-ter-NAH-shuh-nul)—involving many countries.

Major League Soccer (MLS)—the professional soccer league of the United States, started in 1996.

professional (pro-FEH-shuh-nul)—someone who is paid to perform.

qualifying (KWAH-lih-fye-ing)—making the cut to compete in a high-level game or tournament.

quarterfinals (KWAR-ter-FYE-nals)—the part of tournament that determines who will stay to play in the next round.

racism (RAY-sizm)—showing hatred or disrespect toward someone because of the person's race or skin color.

tournament (TUR-nah-ment)—a competition with a series of games to eventually declare a winner, or champion.

under-16, under-17, under-20 teams—teams made up of athletes who are under the age of 16, 17, or 20.

volley—a technique used in soccer for kicking the ball while it's in the air before it touches the ground.

World Cup—the international tournament for outdoor soccer.

Books

Arnold, Caroline. *Soccer.* New York: Franklin Watts, 1991.

Hornby, Hugh. *Soccer.* New York: Dorling Kindersley, 2000.

Magazine Articles

Bradley, Jeff. "DaMarcus Beasley." *Soccer Jr.,* vol. 10, issue 5, November 2001.

Cosgrove, Ellen. "DaMarcus Beasley." *Sports Illustrated for Kids,* vol. 14, issue 10, October 2002.

Howard, Martin. "[Big] Time Players." *Boys Life,* May 2004.

Lisi, Clemente. "Inner-city Blues." *Soccer Digest,* vol. 25, issue 5, December 2002.

Mahoney, Ridge. "Beasley OK with Going Dutch." *USA Today,* September 2, 2004.

Slania, John T. "DaMarcus Beasley." *Chicago Business,* February 28, 2005.

Wahl, Grant. "Home Bodies." *Sports Illustrated,* vol. 92, issue 12, March 20, 2000.

Whiteside, Kelly. "American Player a Stylish Fit with Top Dutch Soccer Team." *USA Today,* April 26, 2005.

Web Addresses

Biography: DaMarcus Beasley, U.S. Soccer,
www.ussoccer.com/bio/
   bio.sps?iBiographyID=1722
Player Bio: DaMarcus Beasley, U.S. Soccer
   Players, www.ussoccerplayers.com/players/
   damarcus_beasley/
PSV
english.psv.nl
U.S. Soccer
www.ussoccer.com
U.S. Soccer Players
www.ussoccerplayers.com

Works Consulted

"About His Biggest Wish and Homesickness,"
   english.psv.nl/show?id=9720&contentid=7823,
   December 7, 2004.
Hornby, Hugh. *Soccer.* New York: Dorling
   Kindersley, 2000.
Interview with Diane Small, Bradenton Preparatory
   Academy, April 12, 2005.
Slania, John T. "DaMarcus Beasley." *Chicago
   Business,* February 28, 2005.
Starr, Mark. "Goooooooooooooal!" *Newsweek,*
   November 18, 2002.

Beasley, DaMarcus
    awards   8, 11, 12, 14, 16, 19
    birth   7
    brother   5, 6, 9, 16
    dreams   6, 7, 12, 17, 19, 20, 25
    family   5, 6, 7
    graduation   12
    high school team   9, 11, 12
    in Florida   8, 9
    in Netherlands   22
    Major League Soccer
        contract   12, 15
    nicknames   25
    parents   5, 6, 24
    racism   23
    with Chicago Fire   13
Beasley, Henry   5, 6
Beasley, Jamar   5, 6, 9, 16, 17
Beasley, Joetta   6
Best XI award   14, 16
Bradenton (Preparatory)
    Academy   8, 10, 12
Chicago (Illinois) Fire   13, 15, 16
Choi, Jin Cheul   18
CONCACAF   19, 22
Donovan, Landon   11
Europe   6, 16, 20, 23
FIFA World Cup   11, 18, 19, 20, 21
Florida Soccer Player of the
    Year   12
Football   22, 23
Fort Wayne, Indiana   7
France   9
French National Soccer   7

Germany   20
International Management Group
    (IMG)   10
International   6, 9
Jones, Cobi   20, 21
Los Angeles (California)
    Galaxy   15
Major League Soccer (MLS)   15, 16
Major League Soccer (MLS) All-
    Star Team   16
Man of the Match Award   11
Midfielder   16
Murawski, Maciej   21
Netherlands   22, 23, 24
Nickelodeon   12
NSCAA High School All-America
    Team   12
Parade All-American High School
    Co-Player of the Year   12
Platini, Michel   7
Poland   21
Pope, Eddie   20, 21
Portugal   20
Professional   7
PSV Eindhoven   22, 23, 24, 25
Racism   23
Sanneh, Tony   20, 21
Silver Ball Award   11
South Korea   18, 20
South Side High School   9
U.S. Under-16 National Team   9
U.S. Under-17 National
    Team   10, 11
U.S. Under-20 National Team   19
World Soccer magazine   16